Coping™

COPING WITH

SEXUAL CONSENT

Erin Staley

Rosen
YA™

New York

Published in 2020 by The Rosen Publishing Group, Inc.
29 East 21st Street, New York, NY 10010

First Edition

Library of Congress Cataloging-in-Publication Data

Names: Staley, Erin, author.
Title: Coping with sexual consent / Erin Staley.
Description: First edition. | New York: Rosen Publishing, 2020. | Series: Coping | Includes bibliographical references and index.
Identifiers: LCCN 2018048167| ISBN 9781508187431 (library bound) | ISBN 9781508187424 (pbk.)
Subjects: LCSH: Sex crimes—Juvenile literature. | Sexual abuse victims—Juvenile literature. | Sexual consent—Juvenile literature.
Classification: LCC HV6556 .S73 2020 | DDC 613.6—dc23
LC record available at https://lccn.loc.gov/2018048167

Manufactured in China

For many of the images in this book, the people photographed are models. The depictions do not imply actual situations or events.

CONTENTS

INTRODUCTION

"Our lives begin to end the day we become silent about things that matter," said Reverend Martin Luther King Jr. in 1965. It was during an era when African Americans were fighting for equality for all, as noted in the US Constitution. Activists, including King, stood together and spoke out for equal opportunity, access to public facilities, the right to vote, and freedom from discrimination. Their efforts paid off as civil rights were extended to all citizens under the law.

In 2017, women spoke out for their right to be free from all forms of sexual violence. That October, the *New York Times* published a harrowing report that detailed decades of sexual harassment allegations from dozens of women against powerful film producer Harvey Weinstein. He was just one of many high-profile men who had robbed others of their right to give or deny sexual consent. Weinstein's arrest become a monumental moment for anti-sexual harassment and assault movements, such as #MeToo and Time's Up.

Legions of empowered women and youths, and some men, began to speak out as well. Allegations

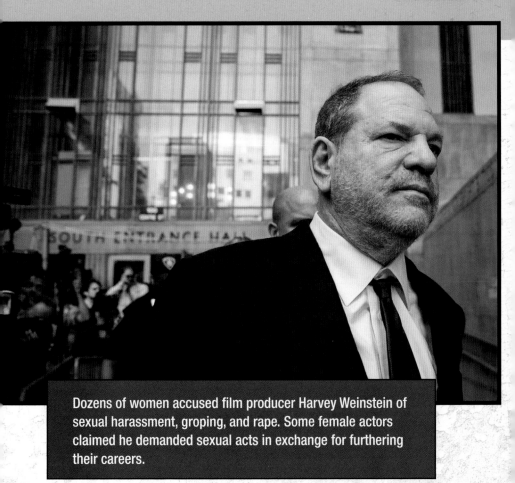

Dozens of women accused film producer Harvey Weinstein of sexual harassment, groping, and rape. Some female actors claimed he demanded sexual acts in exchange for furthering their careers.

of sexual violence—an umbrella term for sexual harassment and sexual assault—spread across national news reports and global social media platforms. Men were publicly called out for all sorts of sexual violence allegations, such as comic Louis C. K., entertainer Kevin Spacey, chef Mario Batali, editor Lorin Stein, conductor James Levine,

Actress Lupita Nyong'o supports the Time's Up movement by wearing all black and a Time's Up pin to the 2018 British Academy of Film and Television Arts Awards after party.

television anchor Matt Lauer, television journalist Charlie Rose, hip-hop mogul Russell Simmons, senator Al Franken, and US president Donald Trump. Survivors' personal stories ignited a new level of awareness around sex, power, and legal consequences. Gone were the days, years, and decades that sexual violence was permitted to persist and then hushed up. Too many survivors were speaking up and prompting new questions about the definition of sexual violence, what resources were available, and how to get justice. Survivors' stories also turned the focus to how far-reaching sexual violence truly is and how global citizens are greatly affected when sexual consent is not given.

Millions have shared their #MeToo experiences via social media. They have also spoken out against all forms of sexual violence at #MeToo rallies, including this one in Tokyo, Japan.

The effects of sexual violence on a survivor are traumatic and life altering. It affects the mind, body, and spirit, leaving survivors to deal with a visible and invisible aftermath. Bruises and broken bones may heal, but the mental and emotional pain can be long lasting. Too often, survivors feel alone and believe that society blames them for what happened.

But this isn't true. They are not alone, and they are not at fault. Survivors, allies, and advocates for sexual consent believe and support them. There are people ready to speak up for survivor rights to access support, resources, and justice. Readers will discover how they, too, can join this movement against sexual violence. They will learn how to cope with assault, how and where to seek help for healing, and how to put an end to a rape culture and victim blaming. Finally, readers will be encouraged to become allies who create safe spaces, and advocates who speak out for things that matter regarding the right to sexual consent for every global citizen.

A Culture of Consent

Sexual consent is the voluntary, conscious, and enthusiastic affirmation to mutually engage in an expression of desire or sexual activity with another person. Excitement must always be present, and each partner must be completely engaged in the experience—or series of experiences—without hesitation. Each partner has the right to give sexual consent, regardless of whether they are in casual or committed monogamous or polyamorous relationships. Each partner has the right to say who can caress, hug, kiss, and tickle their bodies, as well as who they want to engage with during anal, oral, or vaginal sex—without exception. Sexual consent is an ongoing process that can change at any time, regardless of of whether consent was given previously for other individual expressions of desire or sexual activities.

Healthy relationships foster a shared respect for sexual consent. Partners are comfortable in the safe and inclusive space they've created and are supported when they share their struggles.

How to Ask for Sexual Consent

Asking for sexual consent might feel a little awkward, but it demonstrates respect for others. Requests can be simple, sincere, and without pressure. Below are some prompts for asking for sexual consent:

- Are you okay with this?
- Does this feel good?

- What touches do you like?
- Do you want to go further?
- I would like to give you a massage. Would you be into that?
- I would like a massage. Would you be into that?
- Is it OK if I take your shirt off?
- What is your favorite safe word?
- What excites you and/or turns you on?
- Do you have any trigger points?

Author Michael Ellsberg suggests asking about consent early in the encounter. In his article "Affirmative Consent and Erotic Tension," he recommends the following:

I'm attracted to you, and I want to feel free to express my desire with you. And, I'm committed to you feeling totally safe and comfortable with me. So if anything I do with you tonight makes you feel even slightly uncomfortable, I want you to say "Stop" or "Slow down" immediately and I'll stop or slow down.

Verbal and Nonverbal Sexual Consent

Sexual consent is given with a "yes" or positive response, such as "That feels good," "I like to be touched there," or "I'm willing to try." It is also given with nonverbal, physical cues that are voluntary, conscious, and enthusiastic. Nonverbal cues can

Everyone has his or her own level of comfort when it comes to intimacy. It is important to read your partner(s) carefully and ask for sexual consent.

include smiling, laughing, leaning in a little closer, sighing with pleasure, and returning a kiss or touch that is similar to what was offered. Proceed with caution when using nonverbal cues alone to determine whether someone has given sexual consent. Experience is needed to accurately read the other person and the situation as a whole. For example, if two people are hanging out, and the eye contact and smiles are frequent, one might offer a gentle, nonsexual touch to see how the other responds. This can be a light hand on an arm or a soft knee graze. If the other person hesitates, recoils, or seems unresponsive, this means "no," and the touch should stop there. The initiator can then share a compassionate response, such as, "I'm sensing that I've made you hesitant/uncomfortable. We can avoid that altogether, or you can take some time to consider it for another time. The choice is yours completely, and I will respect whatever you decide." If one is confident that the nonverbal cues are giving voluntary, conscious, and enthusiastic consent, the activity can continue. It can also be a single gesture, which can be later explored. To be absolutely sure, both verbal and nonverbal consent should be given simultaneously.

"Blanket Consent" and Safe Words

Sex educator Kenneth Play suggests "blanket consent" as a way to ask for sexual consent. This approach is for experienced partners who know what they like and want sexually and who are comfortable with asking for sexual consent. In a *Teen Vogue* article, sex researcher, writer, and educator Zhana Vrangalova folds blanket consent into this request for consent:

> I'd like the freedom to hook up without continually asking permission for each individual act. But consent is really important to me, so I'd like you to tell me if something doesn't feel good, if you want me to slow down or stop. Does this work for you? Do you feel comfortable saying "no" when you want to say "no"? Or would you rather me check in with you more regularly? Totally cool either way.

Some partners use safe words to set boundaries on how far they want to progress sexually. If a safe word is said, all activity must stop. Safe words can be folded into Vrangalova's suggested request. Selecting your safe word can be fun and shared with a partner. Consider words that represent foods, movie titles, or your favorite song. Some partners use sounds, such as humming or snapping their fingers. You can also use colors like traffic lights: green for "go," yellow for "proceed with caution," and red for "stop."

Saying and Respecting the "No"

Everyone has the right to say "no" to anyone, anytime, for any reason. If you're not comfortable, give a firm "no." This is a strong response and isn't always easy to say. If this is too strong for the situation, soften it by saying, "I like this, but not that," "I don't want to do that, but thanks for asking," or "No, I'm not into doing that." Include nonverbal cues, such as pulling away or moving a hand. Remember to be clear to avoid any confusion. Saying "no" might also feel awkward if you are attracted to the initiator. You may not want to disappoint, upset, or drive a potential partner away. Avoid moving beyond personal boundaries for the wants and needs of another. Stay true to your levels of comfortability.

A survivor might be tempted to confront a sexual violence perpetrator. But this could lead to more harm. Consult with a law enforcement officer, lawyer, advocate, or therapist for help.

One way to get around any awkwardness is to share preferences for asking and giving sexual consent. If blanket consent is preferred, let that be known. If requests for verbal sexual consent should be made with every escalation, say so. If things are escalating and you are not sure about continuing, pause things by saying, "Let's talk first. Then I can decide if I want to go further," or "If I choose to say 'no,' we'll stop what we're doing." Another way to get around awkwardness is to let the other person know what level of comfort exists. For example, if kissing is a new experience, let the other person know. If kissing should be the only activity at this time, say so.

If additional expressions and activities are welcomed, offer something like, "If you're into it, I'd like to kiss and touch your breasts/buttocks/genitals."

It may be disappointing or hurtful to receive a "no" from someone, but avoid the temptation to develop an attitude or pressure the person into doing something he or she doesn't want to do. The "no" may not have anything to do with you. Instead, it may be based in past experiences or the need for personal space or privacy. Just as you have a right to your personal boundaries, so do others. They do not owe you anything.

If It's Not Sexual Consent, What Is It?

If sexual consent is not given and an expression of desire or a sexual act is performed, it's considered to be nonconsensual. Nonconsensual activity is a form of sexual violence. Sexual violence is an umbrella term for various types of sexual harassment and sexual assault. Sexual harassment and sexual assault are abuses of power, disrespect, and disregard for human dignity. The US Equal Employment Opportunity Commission defines sexual harassment as "unwelcome sexual advances, requests for sexual favors, and other verbal or physical harassment of a sexual nature." Under US federal law, sexual harassment is illegal in every state. As a civil violation, it is a form of discrimination that is prohibited by the Civil Rights Act of 1964.

Sexual assault encompasses all forms of unwanted sexual contact with intimate body parts, such as the anus, breast, buttocks, genitalia, groin, and lips. It matters not if the body part is clothed or naked. According to the National Coalition Against Domestic Violence's (NCADV) "National Statistics" article, one in four women and one in six men are sexually assaulted in their lifetimes. Sexual harassment and sexual assault can happen to anyone, anywhere, anytime, and by anyone. The US Department of Justice defines sexual assault as "any type of sexual contact or behavior that occurs without the explicit consent of the recipient. Falling under the definition of sexual assault are sexual activities as forced sexual intercourse, forcible

Law enforcement officers work to respond to and prevent acts of sexual violence, as well as provide information, resources, and support through the criminal-justice process.

sodomy, child molestation, incest, fondling, and attempted rape." Under US federal and state laws, all forms of sexual assault are criminal. States vary on how they are defined and punished.

Myths & FACTS

Myth: Sexual consent, once given, is permanent and applies to all acts.

Fact: A person can change his or her mind at any time. This includes saying "no" to activities that once were consensual. Any expression or activity that continues is considered to be an act(s) of sexual violence. Plus, sexual consent must be given for every individual act. For example, if consent was given for a kiss, it does not mean that sexual consent is given for sex.

Myth: Sexual violence is only committed by strangers.

Fact: The Government of Canada's Department of Justice reports that survivors of sexual assault know the offender in about 80 percent of cases. Perpetrators— those who commit harmful, illegal, or immoral acts—can be boyfriends, girlfriends, spouses, family members, law enforcement, neighbors, school officials, and spiritual leaders.

Myth: If a person is under the influence of alcohol and/or drugs, then sexual consent is not needed.

Fact: A person who is voluntarily or involuntarily high, drunk, vomiting, asleep, or unconscious cannot give sexual consent. Incapacitation could be because of alcohol and/or date rape, prescription, over-the-counter, or recreational drugs. These substances hinder the ability to say "no" or to remember what happened. Rohypnol, ketamine, and gamma-hydroxybutyrate (GHB) are date rape drugs and can be slipped into someone's drink. Since they don't alter the color, flavor, or smell of drinks, they are difficult to detect. Prescription drugs include anxiety medications, muscle relaxers, sleep aids, and tranquilizers. Alcohol, cannabis, cocaine, methamphetamines, heroin, opium, and phencyclidine (PCP) are recreational drugs. They alter one's consciousness, making it difficult to make informed, rational judgments regarding consent.

CHAPTER TWO

The Different Types of Sexual Violence

There are many forms of sexual violence, and each degrades survivors and society in general. From cyber harassment to partner violence, it is important to understand what is happening and what you can do to help yourself and others.

Understanding Cyber Harassment

Cyber harassment, also known as online harassment, is the public sharing of embarrassing, humiliating, offensive material online, resulting in shaming and sustained harassment online.

If you experience online sexual violence, document everything. Take screenshots of call histories, emails, texts, and social media posts. This evidence will help if you press charges.

Examples include name-calling, physical threats, pressuring someone to send nude photos, stalking, and sexual harassment via apps, emails, gaming forums, phone and text messages, social media posts, and websites. Cyber harassment also includes revenge porn, the sharing of sexually explicit photos and videos without someone's consent.

What Is Groping?

Groping is unwanted touching or fondling of someone's breasts, genitals, and buttocks. This happened to award-winning singer and songwriter Taylor Swift. Swift claimed that during a photo op in Denver for her 2013 *Red* tour, radio DJ David Mueller reached under her skirt and grabbed her buttocks. She reported the incident, and Mueller was immediately removed from the concert and later fired. In 2015, Mueller sued the singer for defamation. He sought millions in damages. Swift countersued for assault and battery, and she asked for one dollar in hopes that her stand against sexual harrassment would inspire others. Swift won her case.

Ashley Judd Takes on Cyber Harassment

Actor, activist, and sexual assault survivor Ashley Judd speaks out often about online gender-based violence and misogyny. While attending a University of Kentucky basketball game in 2015, she posted a Twitter comment about the opposing team playing dirty. Hateful online responses flooded in, including degrading sexual names, rape threats, and insults to her appearance, intelligence, and family. Judd acknowledges that what happened

Activist and actor Ashley Judd spoke at the Women's March on Washington in 2017, where she delivered the poem "Nasty Woman," written by nineteen-year-old poet Nina Donovan.

to her is universal and that the anonymity of social media seems to give online users an excuse to degrade millions of women and young people every day.

"Online misogyny is a global gender rights tragedy, and it is imperative that it ends," Judd said in her TEDWomen 2016 talk. She shared that she's a daily target since "misogyny and misogynists have amply demonstrated they will dog my every step. My spirituality, my faith, being a hillbilly—I can say that, you can't—all of it is fair game." Judd endured anger and fear and relied on the strength of others to emphatically say "enough" to sexual violence. She has invited citizens, law enforcement, and lawmakers to join her in her efforts.

(continued on the next page)

(continued from the previous page)

To cope with sexual violence, Judd uses positive affirmations or statements of wisdom to strengthen her resolve to think and behave differently. In her TEDWomen talk, she shared that five affirmations offset one negative interaction. She noted that "gratitude in particular—free, available globally anytime, anywhere, to anyone in any dialect—it fires the pregenual anterior cingulate, a watershed part of the brain that floods it with great, good stuff." Judd encouraged audience members to participate in a call-and-response dialogue with her. She said positive affirmations about herself, such as "I am a powerful and strong woman," and they responded with "Yes, you are!" and a standing ovation.

Know the Facts About Intimate Partner Violence

Intimate partner violence is also known as domestic violence, intimate partner rape, marital rape, and spousal rape. It occurs with a boyfriend, girlfriend, or spouse and is often accompanied by emotional, mental, and/or physical abuse. One in three women around the world have been affected by sexual or physical violence by an intimate partner at some point in her lifetime, notes *The Global Status Report on Violence Prevention 2014* from the World Health Organization (WHO). NO MORE's "Know the Facts" web page reports that one in three teens experience sexual or physical abuse or threats from a boyfriend or girlfriend in one year, and one in nine men experience violence from their partners in their lifetime.

The Effects of Rape

Rape is the nonconsensual penetration, whether slight or full, of any part of the body or placement of an object into someone's mouth, vagina, or anus. It can be planned or impromptu, forced or coerced, by an individual or multiple perpetrators. Rape can begin with consent, until one retracts consent and the act continues. According to the NCADV's "National Statistics," one in five women and one in seventy-one men in the United States have been raped in their lifetime. Nearly half of female (46.7 percent) and male (44.9 percent) victims of rape in the United States were raped by an acquaintance. Of these victims, 45.4 percent of women and 29 percent of men were raped by an intimate partner.

If multiple perpetrators are involved, are filming the act, or watching without intervening, each person is guilty of multiperpetrator sexual assault, or "gang rape." This sexually aggressive form of assault is predominantly committed by young men who believe the act reflects their manhood. Gang rape is often associated with gang membership or the moral punishment of those believed to live and behave immorally.

Sexual Coercion: A Leveraging Act

Sexual coercion is the ongoing attempt to engage in sexual activity with a person, even when that person doesn't immediately agree or has refused multiple times. Perpetrators use their relationship with the person as leverage, pestering him or her to do sexual things the person doesn't want to do. They may say, "I need sex because I'm a guy," "If you love me, you'll let me," and "I paid for dinner, and you owe me." Sometimes alcohol and drugs are given to "loosen up" an unwilling participant.

Stalking as Targeted Harassment

Stalking is the repeated act of targeted harassment, typically involving a person who follows another or waits for him or her before and after school, work, or an event. One in six women and one in nineteen men have experienced stalking, reports the Centers for Disease Control and Prevention (CDC). Stalkers can be strangers but are most often known adults, classmates, or significant others. According to the NCADV's "National Statistics," "1 in 7 women and 1 in 18 men have been stalked by an intimate partner during their lifetime to the point in which they felt very fearful or believed that they or someone close to them would be harmed or killed." Stalking can also involve unwanted online or in-person attention in the form of emails, gifts, phone calls, photos, texts, and threats.

Putting an End to the Rape Culture and Victim Blaming

The term "rape culture" describes an environment in which rape and sexual violence against women is normalized. Male sexual aggression is standardized by misogynistic language, jokes, legal jargon, and laws. Advertisements, books, movies, and TV shows glamorize sexual violence, as kisses are stolen, clothes are ripped off, and aggressors "take" what they want. Song lyrics objectify women, saying they want "it" and that date rape drugs make for a fun night.

Women are made to think they are public property and that men have no control over their desires. If victimized by perpetrators, they are made to feel ashamed. They are blamed for what they're wearing, who they hang out with, what they're drinking, and why they didn't resist more. "Social tendency toward victim-blaming reinforces the notion that abuse and assault are acceptable, and allows the perpetrator to defend and continue their actions," notes the Canadian

In 2012, Toronto, Ontario, in Canada was just one of many locations to host an annual Take Back the Night march and rally. Participants stood against sexual, relationship, and domestic violence.

Women's Foundation's "Fact Sheet Sexual Assault and Harassment."

Women and marginalized populations cope with rape culture by assuming they are never safe. They plan their day to avoid coming and going in the dark. They travel in pairs and groups and avoid sketchy neighborhoods. They constantly look over their shoulders, carry car keys in their hands, keep pepper spray handy, and lock the doors as soon they get into their cars, homes, and

(continued on the next page)

31

(continued from the previous page)

businesses. But this doesn't have to be the way things stay. The rape culture and victim blaming can stop by changing the conversation, educating others, and committing to survivor support.

Verbal and Nonverbal Harassment

Verbal harassment involves the use of words to belittle, criticize, embarrass, humiliate, and insult someone. It involves catcalling, spreading rumors, telling offensive jokes, making discriminatory comments about sex or gender, and asking someone repeatedly to go on a date or perform unwanted acts when consent is not given. Nonverbal harassment includes obscene gestures, writing sexually explicit things about someone, and intimidating a victim into not reporting acts of sexual violence.

Why Do Perpetrators Commit Sexual Assault?

Sexual violence stems from the false belief that the needs of one are more important than the needs of another. Perpetrators view victims as unequal. While some perpetrators are female, most are males who buy into the gender inequity that is reflected in cultural norms, entertainment, media, religion, politics, and workplaces. Apparent and covert messaging from these sources convinces perpetrators that they have power over others. This power turns into extreme masculinity, known as hypermasculinity. It encourages a sense of entitlement and impulsiveness.

Perpetrators also commit acts of sexual violence because they harbor forceful sexual fantasies, a preference for impersonal sex, and a fixation on pornography—all of which objectify and devalue others. A *New York Times* article quotes Jacob (last name not given) as saying:

Many people's first exposure to sexuality is porn, which teaches kids that men should be rough, demanding, and that if a girl says no, you just need to try harder to convince her. We need to teach our children (especially boys) the self-control, respect, and communication necessary for healthy intimacy, and do it long before they have devices they can watch porn on.

Sexual violence can affect a survivor's emotional, physical, and psychological health. With the right help and support, one can manage these challenging effects and heal.

Many perpetrators experienced sexual violence as children, either as victims or bystanders. They may have been in emotionally unsupportive homes, or their traumas were left untreated because of poverty, stigma, or a higher value being placed on the family's honor. Untreated abuse and the inability to cope with what happened can lead to ongoing mental health issues.

CHAPTER THREE

The Victims of Sexual Violence

S exual violence happens in every community, regardless of ability, age, education, ethnicity, gender, sexual orientation and expression, and socioeconomic status. It is done by perpetrators who prey on those whom they consider weak and vulnerable.

Women and Children: Vulnerable Populations

Children are the most vulnerable population. They do not always fight back, have trouble putting into words what happened, and are less likely to speak up. The Rape, Abuse & Incest National Network's (RAINN) article "Scope of the Problem:

Singer-songwriter and rape survivor Tori Amos was the first spokesperson for RAINN. She took the first ceremonial phone call for RAINN's National Sexual Assault Hotline in 1994.

Statistics" notes: "A majority of child victims are 12–17. Of victims under the age of 18: 34% of victims of sexual assault and rape are under age 12, and 66% of victims of sexual assault and rape are age 12–17." This devastating problem is worldwide and multigenerational. Of the 133 countries listed by WHO for *The Global Status Report on Violence Prevention 2014,* one in five women around the world reports having been sexually abused as a child. This calculation represents 6.1 billion people and 88 percent of the world's population. Besides the deliberate physical contact or penetration of private areas, sexual assault also occurs when perpetrators expose themselves to a minor, intentionally observe or violate the private behaviors of a minor, take sexually explicit photos or videos, and/or tell sexually explicit stories to a minor online or in person.

Women are also vulnerable. One in three women in the United States have experienced sexual violence with physical contact during their lives, reports the CDC. The Canadian Women's Foundation reports that women "were 10 times more likely than men to be the victim of a police-reported sexual assault" and that "women accounted for 92 percent of victims of police-reported sexual assaults." These statistics may underestimate the issue, since many victims do not report sexual violence. RISE, a national civil rights nonprofit organization, gives a global perspective to the epidemic. It reports that 35 percent of women on earth—about 1.30 billion people—have survived some form of sexual violence.

Men Are Survivors, Too

Sexual violence also affects men. Professional athlete-turned-actor Terry Crews is a survivor. In 2016, he attended a party with his wife and was introduced to Hollywood agent Adam Venit. Venit allegedly grabbed and held Crews's genitals. Crews filed a lawsuit and became an advocate for the Sexual Assault Survivors' Bill of Rights. This legislation would codify rights for reporting survivors, such as having rape kits preserved in all states. In support, Crews testified in front of the Senate Judiciary Committee in 2018 to share what happened to him. According to an ETOnline article, Crews stated:

> *I sit here before you just as an example, because a lot of people don't believe that a person like me could actually be victimized, and what happened to me has happened to many, many other men in Hollywood, and since I came forward with my story I've had thousands and thousands of men come to me and say, "Me too—this is my story."*

The CDC reports that one in six men have experienced sexual violence. RAINN reports that men account for "8% of RAINN's online hotline users under 18 and 18% of callers older than 18." It goes on to state, "Men and boys often discuss sexual abuse that occurred in the past, with 70% of men and boys discussing an event that occurred more than five years ago and 58% of them discussing a repeated event in the past that is no longer occurring." Sexual violence against men and boys, however, is a significant problem worldwide. WHO found that only 5 to 10 percent of men in developed countries report a history of childhood sexual abuse. Experts believe this statistic is grossly underrepresented. Males

If you know any survivors who can't seem to break off contact with a perpetrator, assure them that what's happening isn't their fault. Let them know that you will be there for them.

are less likely to report because of a fear of not being believed or shame over experiencing sexual arousal and possibly an orgasm during the assault.

Marginalized Populations

Marginalized populations are more vulnerable to sexual violence because they are believed to be in a secondary position of societal importance and are not as readily heard if they speak up. People who identify with multiple marginalized populations may experience further victimization. Following are some of the marginalized populations affected by sexual violence.

The Elderly

Elderly citizens are vulnerable to sexual assault because of memory impairment conditions, such as Alzheimer's disease or dementia. They can become confused or think they won't be believed. According to Nursing Home Abuse Guide's "Elder Sexual Abuse" article, 70 percent of elderly survivors reported sexual abuse in nursing homes, and only 30 percent of survivors reported it to authorities. The report points out that perpetrators are primary caregivers (81 percent of the time) and family members.

Incarcerated Populations

Prisoner rape occurs when an act of sexual violence is made by law enforcement, prison officials, soldiers, staff members, or another inmate. It can be used to establish a hierarchy of discipline and respect or to provide sexual relief for high-ranking

Prisoners with mental health issues and those who identify as LGBTQ+ are at higher risk for sexual abuse when incarcerated than the general population.

officials. Prisoner rape is also inflicted on prisoners as a source of entertainment, making prisoners have sex with one another, or as a punishment for those in the LGBTQ+ community. RAINN's "Scope of the Problem: Statistics" article notes that 80,600 inmates are sexually assaulted or raped each year.

Indigenous Peoples

"Sexual assaults account for about 33% of all crimes committed against Aboriginal women, and 10% of all crimes committed against non-Aboriginal women," notes the Canadian Women's Foundation's "Fact Sheet Sexual Assault and Harassment." Similar findings were noted by the Indian Law Resource Center:

More than 4 in 5 American Indian and Alaska Native women have experienced violence, and more than 1 in 2 have experienced sexual violence. Alaska Native women continue to suffer the highest rate of forcible sexual assault and have reported rates of domestic violence up to 10 times higher than in the rest of the United States.

LGBTQ+ Community

LGBTQ+ individuals face higher rates of marginalization, poverty, and stigma. This puts them at risk for higher rates of hate-motivated violence, including sexual assault. Helen Parshall wrote in her "Sexual Assault Awareness Month 2018" article, "The ways in which society both hypersexualizes LGBTQ+ people and stigmatizes our relationships can lead to intimate partner violence that stems from internalized homophobia and shame." Parshall continues by pointing out that almost half of bisexual women have experienced rape, and half of transgender people will experience sexual violence during their lifetime. She states:

Those numbers are even higher for the bisexual and transgender people who are also people of color or people with disabilities, making these groups vulnerable to further disparities that occur at the intersections of ableism, biphobia, racism and transphobia. According to the Youth Risk Behavior Survey, a national survey of high school students, lesbian and bisexual women and gay and bisexual men experienced higher rates of sexual assault than their straight counterparts.

People with Disabilities

"Disabled women experience sexual violence at about three times the rate of non-disabled women," notes the Canadian Women's Foundation's "Fact Sheet Sexual Assault and Harassment." Similar findings were reported in "The Facts Behind the #MeToo Movement: A National Study on Sexual Harassment and Assault." It states:

Persons with disabilities were significantly more likely to experience all forms of sexual harassment and assault than people without disabilities. The strongest findings were for the more severe forms, for physically aggressive sexual harassment (among women, 69% vs 59%, and among men, 39% vs 23%, for those with and without a disability, respectively) and sexual assault (among women, 40% vs 23%, and among men, 18% vs 4%, for those with and without a disability, respectively).

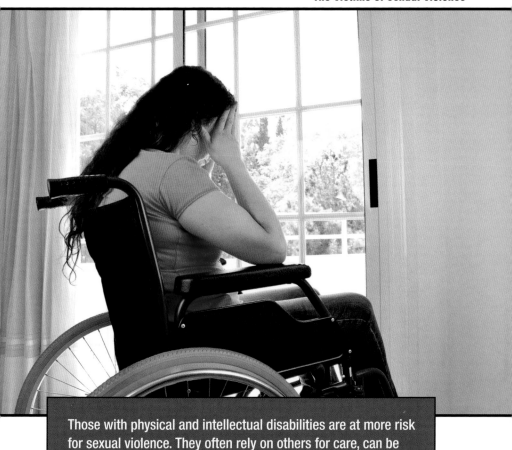

Those with physical and intellectual disabilities are at more risk for sexual violence. They often rely on others for care, can be overpowered physically, and may have trouble communicating.

Refugees and Victims of Armed Conflicts

Rape has long been used as a strategy to subvert community bonds. Syrian refugees are a modern-day example. Peaceful protests on March 15, 2011, turned into violent crackdowns by Syrian security forces. A civil war resulted. The brutal conflict killed

45

hundreds of thousands and tore apart a nation. More than 5.6 million Syrians fled the country and created a massive refugee and displacement crisis. About 6.1 million were displaced within the country, and half of those were youths. They were subjected to loss, physical and psychological trauma, and sexual violence. Even government officials raped women, men, and children to terrorize and punish oppositional communities.

Sex Workers

Sex workers, whether trafficked or not, are at risk for sexual violence. They are vulnerable to ill-willed clients, and if prostitution is illegal in their country, they are less likely go to the police. WHO's "World Report on Violence and Health" states:

> *A survey of female sex workers in Leeds, England, and Glasgow and Edinburgh, Scotland, revealed that 30% had been slapped, punched or kicked by a client while working, 13% had been beaten, 11% had been raped and 22% had experienced an*

attempted rape. Only 34% of those who had suffered violence at the hands of a client reported it to police. A survey of sex workers in Bangladesh revealed that 49% of the women had been raped and 59% beaten by police in the previous year; the men reported much lower levels of violence. In Ethiopia, a study of sex workers also found high rates of physical and sexual violence from clients, especially against the child sex workers.

Undocumented Individuals

Undocumented individuals might not know anyone in their new country, let alone speak the language or communicate with anyone back home. This makes survivors susceptible to perpetrators who threaten to turn them in to the authorities if they do not keep quiet. Threats can include separation from their children, destroyed legal documents, reports to employers, employment dismissal, or a denied petition for legal status.

CHAPTER FOUR

Next Steps to Safety and Treatment

Safety is crucial, and survivors are encouraged to get help by calling 911 in the United States and Canada. For added support, contact a friend, family member, or sexual assault advocate. An advocate is a trained professional or volunteer who offers emotional support, guidance regarding next steps, and resources regarding medical attention. Seeking medical treatment within 120 hours (five days) of a sexual assault is highly recommended. This involves treatment for bleeding, bruises, broken/dislocated bones, soreness, and difficulty walking. Medical treatment can also include a sexual assault forensic exam, which can prove helpful if the decision is made to file a report with law enforcement. Also known as

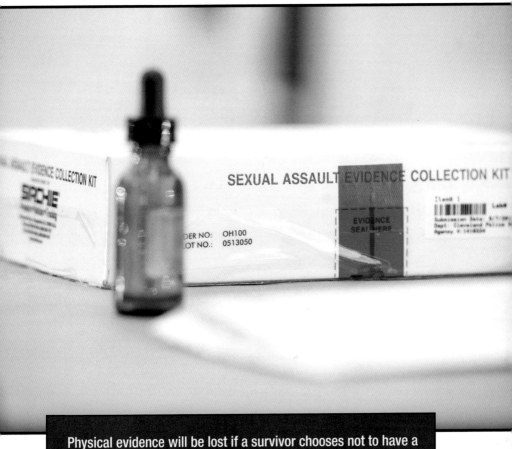

Physical evidence will be lost if a survivor chooses not to have a rape kit. DNA evidence should be collected within seventy-two hours (three days) so that it can be analyzed by a crime lab.

a sexual assault evidence kit or "rape kit," this exam is given by trained personnel who ask for consent during each phase of the process. A loved one or an advocate can accompany a victim, and some hospitals and health care facilities offer advocates for LGBTQ+ and male survivors.

49

How to Prepare for a Sexual Assault Forensic Exam

Following sexual assault, it's natural to want to bathe, brush your teeth, change clothes, clean the crime scene, douche, drink, eat, wash your hands, and/or urinate. Avoid this temptation, since physical evidence can be washed away. Leave everything as is until a sexual assault forensic examiner can be of assistance. Even if you choose not to initiate an investigation now, decisions can change in the future. If you have showered, changed clothes, or cleaned the crime scene, still seek medical attention.

Place clothing and personal belongings worn at the time of the assault in separate paper bags. Avoid plastic bags, since they damage evidence. Used bedding, condoms, and towels can also be bagged. Bring these items to the sexual assault forensic exam. Other forms of evidence can be shared, such as phone/text messages, emails, and/or social media posts sent by the perpetrator. Take screenshots, if possible, and note the names of those who may have seen you before or after the assault. These will help reconstruct a timeline of events if you choose to file a police report and press charges against the perpetrator.

The sexual assault forensic exam takes several hours. Survivors can take a break, stop, or skip a part of the exam. Emergency contraception is given to prevent pregnancy, and tests are given for sexually transmitted infections (STIs). STIs are viruses and bacteria that have been passed via anal, oral, or vaginal contact and can include chlamydia, gonorrhea, hepatitis B, herpes, HIV, human papillomavirus (HPV), and syphilis. A toxicology kit can be requested if drugs were administered— or thought to be administered—by the perpetrator to facilitate the assault. The examiner will give a head-to-toe examination of the anus, genitals, and mouth. Photos of the injured areas on the body may also be taken. Questions about medical history, current medications, preexisting conditions, and any recent consensual sexual activity will be asked.

This will help accurately connect the appropriate deoxyribonucleic acid (DNA) to the perpetrator and not to a consensual partner. DNA is the material in cells that determines characteristics of living things, such as hair and eye color. It is found in blood, saliva, semen, skin tissue, sweat, and urine from the body, clothing, personal belongings, and other objects at the crime scene. Special bags, combs, envelopes, paper sheets, and swabs are used to preserve and collect DNA left behind by the perpetrator. DNA helps prosecutors build a strong court case against known or unknown perpetrators in court.

DNA samples, photos, and personal belongings are then given to law enforcement. If the perpetrator is not known, DNA samples are shared with forensic scientists at a crime lab. Forensic scientists build a profile of the perpetrator and work with law enforcement to compare the DNA of the perpetrator to a national database known as CODIS (the Combined DNA Index System) of already-recorded perpetrators. The Canadian equivalent is the National DNA Data Bank. Suspects can then be identified if they're already in the system, and legal consequences can be pursued. Samples help investigators piece together what happened, especially if the survivor and perpetrator have differing stories, and can help build a strong court case against the perpetrator. In most cases, forensic exams need to be given within seventy-two hours (three days) in order for a crime lab to analyze the DNA evidence. Once the evidence is collected, it is stored for a particular time, depending on the state, province, or territory. After the exam, a follow-up appointment is often scheduled to make sure injuries are healing. Community resources and reporting options may also be offered.

While many hospitals and health care facilities have trained examiners for these exams, some do not. Victims in the United States are encouraged to call the National Sexual Assault Hotline at (800) 656-HOPE (4673) for facility recommendations. Victims in Canada are encouraged to visit Ending Violence at http://endingviolencecanada.org/getting-help for province-based service partners across the country.

The Choice to Report

Survivors have the right to choose whether to report sexual assault to law enforcement, regardless of whether forensic evidence was collected. Reporting can be done to 911, a law enforcement officer, or during a sexual assault forensic exam. The person taking the report is usually a law enforcement officer who has special training in working with survivors of sexual assault. These individuals are often a part of

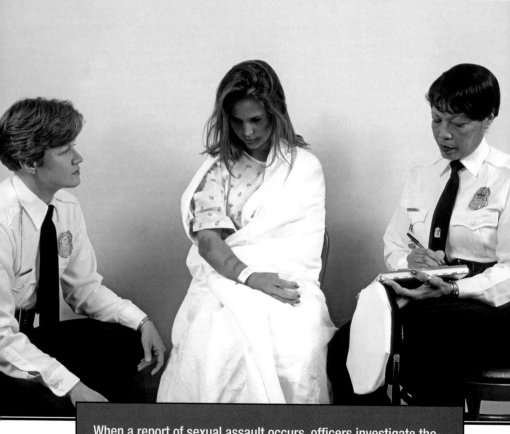

When a report of sexual assault occurs, officers investigate the case and keep the survivor updated. They then decide whether to charge the perpetrator, depending on evidence.

agencies that participate in sexual assault response teams (SARTs). SARTs offer a survivor-focused response after an assault. They are made up of law enforcement agencies, medical personnel, and local sexual assault service providers. They coordinate investigation and communication efforts. If a police report is filed, victims have the right to keep a copy.

"Only 310 out of 1,000 sexual assaults are reported to police," notes RAINN's article "The Criminal Justice System: Statistics," which means approximately two out of three assaults go unreported. The article goes on to state that 20 percent of female university student survivors report, and 32 percent of female nonstudent survivors report. Twenty-eight percent of elderly survivors report; 43 percent of female military survivors report; and 10 percent of male military survivors report. Survivors report to help them recover and regain a sense of control over their lives. Others report to prevent sexual assault from happening to others. In the case of Taylor Swift, she reported to prevent a particular perpetrator from reoffending. Swift is quoted by *Time*'s Eliana Dockterman as saying:

At the time, I was headlining a major arena tour and there were a number of people in the room that saw this plus a photo of it happening. I figured that if he would be brazen enough to assault me under these risky circumstances and high stakes, imagine what he might do to a vulnerable, young artist if given the chance.

A courtroom sketch shows singer-songwriter Taylor Swift on the witness stand during a Denver, Colorado, trial in August 2017. She spoke out to protect others from sexual violence.

Some survivors choose not to report because they know the perpetrator, have been previously intimate with the perpetrator, or don't think there's enough evidence to prove wrongdoing. Some are afraid they won't be believed, will be blamed, or will get into trouble with their parents or the law. They may distrust law enforcement, be concerned that the perpetrator will retaliate, or be pressured by others to keep quiet. But survivors also have the right to remain confidential. Names, residences, and contact information will be kept from being disclosed publicly.

Working with the Statute of Limitations

The choice to report is up to the survivor, but there may be a window of time that the state, province, or territory has to charge the perpetrator. This is called a statute of limitations. It begins when the crime occurs and ends at the predetermined time set by state legislators. Statutes of limitations were designed to discourage convictions that were built on unreliable witness testimony, such as memories of past events. In modern days, however, DNA evidence, audio/video recordings, emails, and text messages are undeniable and strengthen criminal cases against perpetrators. Every state's statute of limitations differs, even if the sexual assault acts are the same. For example, one state can have an unlimited statute of limitations for rape, which means that prosecutors can bring charges against a suspect at any time. Another state could have a fifteen-year statute of limitations for the same act, preventing charges in year sixteen and onward.

What It Means to Press Charges

Sexual assault is illegal in the United States and Canada, but the definitions of each act, legal procedures, legislation, and severity of penalties for convicted perpetrators vary among states and provinces. This is also true for other countries. Sexual assault advocates, survivor support organizations, and attorneys who specialize in sexual violence cases can assist you in navigating the process as it pertains to your situation.

Once a report is made, it's up state law enforcement or a prosecutor to determine whether there is enough evidence—or whether the perpetrator can be identified—to press criminal charges. Cases can often be resolved with a plea bargain, in which survivors don't need to testify. Perpetrators plead guilty in exchange for reduced penalties, such as lighter sentencing. Cases can also be resolved in criminal court, which means survivors may need to testify. Some state and federal laws have built-in ways to protect survivors who participate in trials. A rape shield law is one example. It puts limitations on what the defense can ask about the survivor's previous sexual history. Some states allow survivors to have an advocate during interviews with the prosecutor and the perpetrator's legal representative, as well as during the trial. This added support helps make the process less intimidating.

Survivors have rights when it comes to prosecution, including the right to receive notification of a plea agreement, to receive witness fees and mileage reimbursement, and to take time away from work to testify. If one opts to attend court proceedings and sentencing, he or she can have an advocate present.

A victim impact statement can be made, and the survivor can have any assault details removed from his or her sexual history. As the case progresses, survivors have the right to receive notifications on parole hearings and information on the release, escape, recapture, or death of the perpetrator.

Realistic Expectations and Outcomes

According to RAINN's "The Criminal Justice System: Statistics," only thirteen cases out of every thousand instances of rape are referred to a prosecutor, and only seven lead to a felony conviction. Plus, the pursuit of justice can take a toll on the survivor's mind, body, and resources. *Time*'s Eliana Dockterman shares Taylor Swift's observation:

> *Going to court to confront this type of behavior is a lonely and draining experience, even when you win, even when you have the financial ability to defend yourself. Even though awareness is higher than ever about workplace sexual harassment, there are still so*

many people who feel victimized, afraid and silenced by their abusers and circumstances. When the jury found in my favor, the man who sexually assaulted me was court-ordered to give me a symbolic $1. To this day he has not paid me that dollar, and I think that act of defiance is symbolic in itself.

Former Michigan State University and USA Gymnastics doctor Larry Nassar was sentenced to 40 to 175 years in prison for multiple counts of criminal sexual conduct.

It is a challenge, but regardless of the outcome, reporting will increase the chances the perpetrator will eventually be caught and made to face legal consequences. If the desired outcome is not possible within the criminal justice system, a civil suit can be filed. This is a lawsuit in civil court that awards monetary compensation.

Entitled to Financial Compensation

Survivors have the right to receive direct financial compensation from a state agency, if the crime is reported within a predetermined amount of time—usually seventy-two hours. Maximum compensation benefits vary by state and help cover attorney fees, emergencies, lost wages, medical costs, mental health counseling, moving expenses (when recommended by police or therapists), rehabilitation, and funerals following a sexual assault. Funds often come from convicted perpetrators who are court ordered to pay court fees and through the federal Victims of Crime

Act, which was enacted in 1984. The application process varies per state but typically requires the survivor to submit an application to the state agency between 180 days and two years following the crime. Medical bills, a police report, and other relevant documents are needed to support the claim.

CHAPTER FIVE

The Healing Journey

Sexual assault is traumatizing to the physical body and even more so to the mind and emotions. Visible and invisible effects can be immediate and long lasting, and they are different for every survivor. Visible effects include physical injuries, but these will heal as the body rejuvenates itself. One survivor named L. M. offers this wisdom: "Today in science class I learned every cell in our entire body is replaced every seven years. How lovely it is to know one day I will have a body you will never have touched."

The Invisible Effects of Sexual Violence

The US Department of Veterans Affairs reports that 94 percent of female survivors experience post-traumatic stress disorder (PTSD) during the two weeks following the assault. They have a hard time adjusting or coping, which can lead to severe anxiety, fear, flashbacks, nightmares, and uncontrollable thoughts. Thirty percent continue to experience PTSD symptoms nine months afterward. Depression can cause crying, feelings of hopelessness, lethargy, prolonged sadness, drastic weight changes, and a loss of interest in activities and hobbies that were once enjoyable. Dissociation is a defense mechanism that one contrives to deal with the trauma caused by sexual violence. It includes an inability to be present in the moment or to focus on academics, work, and other activities.

Prolonged mental and emotional trauma can lead to eating disorders, self-harm, sexual dysfunction, and sleep disorders. Survivors may try to cope with self-destructive behaviors, like substance abuse, self-harm, and suicide. RAINN reports that 33 percent of survivors consider suicide, and 13 percent attempt it. To avoid prolonging the effects of untreated mental and emotional trauma, survivors can reach out to advocates and sexual assault survivor organizations for help. This is a sign of strength and means that you are making decisions to begin a journey of healing. Survivors can be encouraged by the words of author, poet, and civil rights activist Maya Angelou: "I can be changed by what happens to me, but I refuse to be reduced by it."

It's OK to Feel What You're Feeling

If you're angry, be angry. If you're sad, be sad. If you're happy, enjoy every moment of those feel-good emotions. Ranges in feelings are a normal part of the process of recovery and healing. In fact, this personal journey is cyclical in nature, with good and bad days. Jennifer Rollin writes in her *Psychology Today* article:

There are many stages of healing following a trauma, and everyone copes with this process differently. It's important to note that healing and coping with the impact of trauma can take time, but it is completely possible to get to a place where you are able to have healthy relationships, rebuild a sense of trust and security, and find meaning and purpose in your life.

Long-Term Healing with Therapy

Trauma can affect the brain after sexual assault. A trained and objective therapist can help survivors navigate experiences and troubling emotions. These include clinical social worker/therapists, psychiatrists, psychologists, and psychotherapists.

Emotional distress and mental illness occur when individuals experience ongoing (even occasional) threats and unsafe conditions that are not addressed and treated.

Help can also come from certified peer specialists who have experienced sexual assault themselves. They are trained and certified to provide guidance and mentoring. Social workers help with case management and resource referrals. Pastoral counselors are trained clergy members who are members of the Association of Pastoral Counselors. Their training is equivalent to a doctorate in counseling. While therapy techniques vary, therapists offer compassionate support to help you process what happened and develop strategies to handle triggers when they occur. In general, therapy sessions are confidential, and anything you need to say will stay between you and your therapist or counselor. By law, this confidentiality agreement can only be broken if you are believed to be a danger to yourself or others. Law enforcement or a family member could be notified.

To find a qualified, highly respected therapist, ask for a referral from an advocate, guidance counselor, insurance agent, medical professional, or spiritual leader. *Psychology Today* offers a Find a Sexual Abuse Therapist tool for those looking for therapists, treatment centers, and support groups in Canada and the United States. Online help is also available. Crisis Text Line offers free, 24/7 text support and information to users who are facing any type of crisis. Users can text "HOME" to 741741 from anywhere in the United States. A trained crisis counselor volunteer will respond with support. The organization 7 Cups offers free, anonymous, and confidential online text chats with volunteer listeners, online therapists, and counselors.

Coping with Triggers

Triggers are disruptive reminders and flashbacks of trauma that pop up in everyday life. They are very common and vary per survivor. Examples include hearing the song that was playing during the assault or smelling a scent worn by a perpetrator. Triggered states can involve anger, anxiety, bitterness, frustration, and sadness. They can also make you feel as if you aren't seen or heard or that your thoughts and opinions aren't valid. Emotional swings, desires to commit self-harm, and feeling unbalanced or being on "high alert" are not uncommon. With therapy, though, triggers can become less frequent and intense. Therefore offers a safe, structured environment in which survivors learn to recognize and develop strategies to cope with triggers.

Love Yourself with Self-Care

Self-care is about learning to love yourself despite sexual assault. You are so much more than the decisions and actions of others. You matter. You are valuable. And you are believed. As you recover and heal, care for your basic needs. Get plenty of rest—a recommended nine to nine and a half hours per night for teenagers. Sleep boosts mood, lowers depression, and repairs the body. Eat healthy, nutrient-rich foods and drink plenty of water to accelerate healing and overcome anxiety. Slow the mind and relax the body with meditation and deep breathing. Deepen your faith system. Release feel-good endorphins— natural chemicals made by the body—with laughter and exercise. Express yourself through journaling, painting, sculpture, and theater. Then get involved. Join a friend in learning a new skill, trying a fun new culinary dish, or doing an impromptu dance to your

Allies make a difference. They listen. They ask what they can do to help. And they assure survivors that they will unconditionally support their decisions during the healing journey.

favorite song. You can also volunteer to help others. Donate, give blood, or bake "just because" brownies to surprise a loved one.

Safety Apps for Mobile Devices

Mobile apps can keep you safe. Designed by survivors and their allies, the myPlan app lets users identify and navigate abusive relationships. It offers personalized safety planning options, resources, and direction regarding unhealthy relationships, as well as tools to make informed decisions about treatment options. myPlan's Campus Toolkit features free resources that help student leaders, school administrators, faculty, and staff support survivors and promote school and campus safety.

Another app, bSafe, allows users to customize a security network from the contacts list on their mobile device. This network of "Guardians" is made up of the people listed in the user's contact list. Guardians can check in on your safety, monitor you via a built-in map, and vocally activate an alarm if you can't get to your phone. If the SOS button is activated, they will receive alerts to your Global Positioning System (GPS) location. Guardians can even view what's happening via live video streaming. The streaming can be recorded,

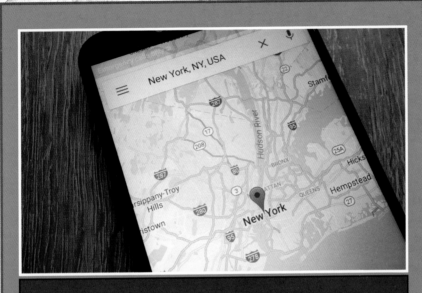

Protect yourself by making sure your online settings and passwords are private. Safeguard your personal computer, mobile devices, internet connection, and social media platforms.

which could help strengthen a case in court. Users can send their location to a friend for a pickup or use a fake phone call to remove themselves from uncomfortable situations.

Healthy and Unhealthy Relationships

Everyone deserves to be in a healthy relationship. In a healthy relationship, participants accept personal differences and boundaries. They appreciate time together but also spend time individually and with others. They act fairly and with respect to one another's thoughts, feelings, belongings, money, resources, responsibilities, and safety. Those in healthy relationships communicate openly and honestly, without threatening words or actions. When disagreements arise, which is a part of healthy relationships, they are respectful, talk things through, and reach compromises. Unhealthy relationships—also known as dating violence, domestic violence, intimate partner violence, and relationship violence—are the opposite. Partners in unhealthy relationships use words and behaviors to control, intimidate, and harm each other. Below are signs and symptoms of unhealthy relationships:

1. Economic demands that cause one to become financially dependent or preventing a partner from going to work or school.
2. Electronic demands that give access to emails, social media accounts, and phone and text messages.

3. Emotional abuse that undermines a person's abilities, achievements, appearance, intelligence, relationships with others, and self-esteem.

4. Physical abuse that includes biting, choking, the denial of medical care, forced substance use/abuse, grabbing, hair pulling, hitting, pinching, pushing, slapping, and yelling.

5. Psychological abuse that involves fear with intimidation, forced isolation from loved ones and activities, and threats of harm to others, pets, and property.

6. Sexual violence with nonconsensual words and actions.

7. Threats using gestures, weapons, and words to injure or disable.

If you suspect a relationship is unhealthy, consult a therapist or trusted friend. An online quiz by Loveisrespect can also help. Look for "Quiz: Is my relationship healthy?," "Quiz: Am I a good partner?," and "Quiz: Can abusers change?"

Being Safe and Social

An active social life is an important part of maturing. It boosts self-esteem, helps improve social and emotional skills, and lowers feelings of isolation. Take safety measures while enjoying the fun. Tell others where you're going, who you're traveling with, and what time you plan to arrive and return. Write your friend's number in permanent marker on your arm, in case you get separated or your mobile device loses power. If you're driving, park in a well-lit location and lock the doors, then stay alert to what's going on around you and your friends. Trust your instincts, and remove yourself if you feel unsafe.

When possible, avoid alcohol and drugs. These substances impair judgment and leave you vulnerable to injury or assault. If you do choose to drink, eat a full meal ahead of time. Know your limits, and alternate alcoholic drinks with 8 ounces (236.6 milliliters) of water. This will help maintain hydration, which improves mental capacity. Drink only from presealed beverages or those you pour yourself. Watch your beverage at all times, and get a fresh one if you set it down. Keep a trusted, sober

Healthy relationships, whether romantic or not, help reduce psychological stress, promote physical healing and healthy behaviors, and give participants a greater sense of well-being.

friend with you at all times. Apply this same advice if you choose to take drugs. Make sure substances come from trusted sources. When you're ready to leave, go with a trusted, sober friend, a designated driver, or ride-sharing service. If you're leaving with a new friend, let others know who it is, where you're going, and when you plan to return.

Before going on a date, share the details of your plan with loved ones. Check in with phone calls and text messages (never use social media platforms). While on the date, clearly communicate that you will give and ask for consent before engaging in any sexual behavior. If you initiate a light touch on the arm, never assume you've been given sexual consent if your potential partner is passive, silent, or accompanies you to a private location. Pay attention to verbal and nonverbal communication, and if your potential partner's words and/or actions aren't clear, pause and have a conversation.

Stay safe and social by making all social media platforms private. Avoid giving out personal details and contact information to strangers or unreliable people. Keep in mind that some apps give others access to track your location in real time via GPS. Should you want to meet up with someone via a social media dating app, choose a public place, such as a café, museum, or sporting event. Invite a friend(s) to come along. If you're going alone, let a trusted friend know where you'll be, who you're with, and when you expect to return.

10 Great Questions to Ask a Therapist

1. How long have you been practicing?

2. Do you have experience working with survivors of trauma, like sexual assault?

3. Have you ever worked with someone from my gender/ethnicity/community?

4. What is your theoretical basis for therapy?

5. How often do you see patients?

6. How long are your therapy sessions?

7. What does a typical session involve?

8. How will I know if I'm making progress?

9. If I'm experiencing an emergency, how should I reach you?

10. What is your fee schedule, and are your services covered by health insurance?

CHAPTER SIX

Allies and Advocates for Sexual Consent

Chances are you know someone who is coping with sexual violence. As an ally, you can make a positive difference by supporting survivors and committing to societal change for sexual consent. Allies understand they don't have to be experts, but friends. When they see something off, they say something. They recognize signs of sexual assault in others, such as eating disorders, depression, pregnancy, self-harm, STIs, substance abuse, or suicide talk or attempts. Allies practice sexual consent within their own relationships and ask for permission to post/tag a friend's photo or video on social media. Allies avoid misogynistic jokes that can be heard by survivors and perpetrators and strive to put an end to rape culture and victim blaming.

If a survivor confides in you, listen without judgment, interruptions, or distractions. This is an important way to show support. Assure her that you believe what she is saying, she is not to blame, and she is not alone. This immediately facilitates the healing process. Convey that anger, anxiety, fear, and/or sadness are normal. Support her in making her own decisions, on her own time, about next steps. Offer help in getting more information about resources, medical treatment, and reporting options, and ask if she'd like company when going to a health care facility, hospital, police department, or survivor support center. Be careful not to impose your own opinions on her decisions, and remember to be respectful of her privacy. Her story is not yours to share, so guard knowledge of the incident and those involved.

Bystander Intervention: See Something, Say Something

A bystander is one who witnesses an act or an attempted act of sexual assault on another. According to the Associated Press, a bystander is present in approximately 30 percent of cases of rape, threats of rape, or nonconsensual sexual contact. But bystanders can intervene by saying something when they see something off. The direct, distract, and delegate strategy is one way to intervene safely and effectively.

1. Be direct—Ask those in distress if they need help with a simple, "Are you OK?" This lets them know you're concerned and are available to help, call someone, or offer a ride.

2. Distract—Distract the perpetrator with a short statement, such as, "Hey, I think your friend is looking for you outside." This pauses the action and gives the person in distress a chance to get away. Or you can say something that removes the person in distress, such as "Can you show me where the restroom is?"

or "I think you dropped your keys back there, and I can show you where they are."

3. Delegate—If the situation is unsafe or you don't know the person in distress, get help from a friend or an authority figure.

Demonstrators took to the streets to protest rape culture in the seventh annual SlutWalk in Jerusalem, Israel, in 2018. They proclaimed that women should be able to wear what they want.

Jump-Start the Conversation

We create the world we want by changing the conversation. If nothing is being said, we can jump-start the conversation. For some survivors, this means sharing their stories. Author and wellness consultant Alex Elle says, "You're not a victim for sharing your story. You are a survivor setting the world on fire with your truth. And you never know who needs your light, your warmth, and raging courage." Many survivors find that going public is validating and offers closure. Some tell those in their circle of influence, while others share with more public venues, such as blogs, newspapers, magazines, social media, and websites. Survivors who share are in control of their stories, offering as much or as little information as they'd like. This bravery raises awareness and results in fewer acts of sexual violence.

Because sexual violence can be a sex-specific act against women, it's important that men create safe spaces for conversation, healing, and outreach. This starts with listening to those with whom you live, learn, and interact. Consider their struggles, what they need, and whether they can trust and safely confide in you. Consider any power and privilege you may have and how it influences your words and behaviors. Engage with antisexist groups and inspire other men to embrace positive role modeling. And if apologies are needed, share them generously and with sincerity. Women, too, can explore these considerations in order to help their boyfriends, brothers, fathers, friends, grandfathers, husbands, neighbors, sons, and uncles.

Advocacy: Elevating Global Consciousness

Advocates for sexual consent speak out for social justice regarding sexual violence. There are many ways to get involved, such as volunteering to become a peer educator in your school and community. Answer hotlines at rape crisis centers. Raise funds to keep rape crisis centers and other organizations that rely on public funding operational. Take part in a Take Back the Night event, in which women from around the world build connections, reclaim their right to safety, and make public declarations against violence in their communities. Host an International Women's Day (every March 8) festivity to celebrate women's struggles and strengths. Or participate in anti-sexual assault movements, such as #MeToo and Time's Up.

#MeToo Movement

After learning about a thirteen-year-old girl who was sexually assaulted by her mother's boyfriend, activist and survivor Tarana Burke founded the Me Too movement in 2006. Burke wanted female survivors—especially women and girls of color—to know they weren't alone. In 2017, a similar heart tug affected actress Alyssa Milano. She'd heard reports about the politicians and Hollywood moguls who committed acts of sexual violence and assault and shared this 2017 Twitter post: "If you've been sexually harassed or assaulted write 'me too' as a reply to this tweet." The phrase became a hashtag and went viral. More than sixty-six thousand users responded with their own stories of sexual violence.

The #MeToo movement turned the spotlight on sexual violence. It opened the conversation to men, women, and children who shared survivor stories and took part in marches and rallies.

Burke then picked up her movement again. She is quoted by *Times*'s Alix Langone as saying, "We are doing it [the #MeToo movement] from a framework that's central to survivors, and to make sure that the most marginalized among survivors have access to resources that will help them cross the human journey." The #MeToo movement is not only a hashtag but a conversation starter that elevates global consciousness. Millions use #MeToo as a way to champion the end of sexual violence and the societal systems that perpetuate it. Today, the #MeToo movement welcomes volunteer efforts to continue its efforts.

Time's Up Movement

In November 2017, a letter of solidarity from the Alianza Nacional de Campesinas (National Farmworkers Women's Alliance) on behalf of seven hundred thousand female farmworkers was written to the women in Hollywood, California, who exposed sexual abuse allegations against Harvey Weinstein. The letter was published and spoke of the farmworkers' own experiences with sexual assault and harassment. In response, more than three hundred actresses, female agents, directors, entertainment executives, producers, and writers wrote their own letter. It pledged support to working-class women confronting sexual harassment and assault, as well as workplace and gender parity issues, like equal pay and equal work environments. The letter

Actor Sandra Bullock wore the Time's Up pin in support of the movement while attending the 90th Annual Academy Awards ceremony in Hollywood, California, in 2018.

appeared as a full-page ad in the *New York Times* and in *La Opinion* (a Spanish-language newspaper). It announced the Time's Up movement on January 1, 2018. Time's Up works to get legislation passed that will free all people to exercise their right to care for themselves and their families and earn a living without discrimination, harassment, and sexual assault. The Time's Up Legal Defense Fund was created to provide financial and legal support for those who fight sexual misconduct via the justice system. Within two months, $21 million was collected. More than two hundred lawyers volunteered their help and resources to assist the one thousand people who requested help from the fund.

Do-It-Yourself Advocacy

Students can be instrumental in creating effective advocacy. While attending a party as a high school freshman at St. Paul's School in New Hampshire, Chessy Prout was raped by senior student Owen Labrie. It took place as part of a school tradition known as the Senior Salute. Seniors were allegedly encouraged to accumulate as many sexual encounters with younger female students as possible. Prout decided to assert her rights as a survivor. The trial against Labrie gained worldwide attention. Prout later went on to create the #IHaveTheRightTo campaign to encourage others to be a positive force of change and to bring safety and respect to all cultures. She went on to write her memoir, *I Have the Right To: A High School Survivor's Story of Sexual Assault, Justice, and Hope.*

Efforts Are Paying Off

Thanks to the combined efforts of survivors, allies, and advocates, many resources and laws have been put into place to prevent sexual violence from harming potential victims. One such survivor is Amanda Nguyen. As a Harvard University senior, Nguyen was raped. She sought help but was met with an inherently broken criminal justice system in Massachusetts. There, survivors had six months to report sexual assault or their rape kits were destroyed, despite the state's fifteen-year statute of limitations. This was not effective in making arrests, and it wasn't consistent with other states in the country. Nguyen decided to rewrite legislature for the civil rights of survivors. She promoted the Sexual Assault Survivors' Bill of Rights, and the US Congress passed it unanimously. Nguyen is the founder of RISE, a national civil rights nonprofit organization. Below are some additional examples of legislation that helps prevent sexual violence while offering some justice for survivors.

The Jeanne Clery Act

The Jeanne Clery Act requires colleges and universities to disclose crime statistics and security policies to students and the general public. It was named in honor of Jeanne Clery, who was in her first year at Lehigh University in Bethlehem, Pennsylvania. In 1986, Josoph Henry gained entry to her dormitory via propped-open doors and randomly selected Clery as a victim. Henry raped and murdered Clery in her dorm room. Clery's parents believed the university's lack of campus security led to the death of their daughter. They sued Lehigh University, saying that Jeanne would not have attended the university if it had publicized the thirty-eight assaults and other violent crimes that occurred on campus over a three-year period. The lawsuit was settled for $2 million. The Clerys used the money to found Security on Campus, a nonprofit organization that advocated for the passage of the Clery Act in 1990. Henry was sentenced to death via the electric chair.

Dru's Law

The Adam Walsh Child Protection and Safety Act was signed into law on July 27, 2006. It included Dru's Law. Among other things, this law changed the name of the National Sex Offender Public Registry to the Dru Sjodin National Sex Offender Public

Website (NSOPW). The NSOPW offers location information on registered sex offenders who live and work in communities, regardless of state boundaries. The NSOPW draws from updated state, territorial, and tribal sex offender registries. The NSOPW also has an app that locates the registered addresses of registered sex offenders within a quarter, half, or full mile of one's mobile device. The NSOPW was named in memory of Dru Sjodin, a college student from North Dakota, who was kidnapped and murdered by sex offender Alfonso Rodriguez Jr. Rodriguez was a Level 3 Minnesota-registered sexual offender. After a twenty-three year prison sentence, he was released and crossed state lines to commit his crime. He was arrested in 2003, found guilty in 2006, and sentenced to death later that same year.

Debbie Smith Act

This act eliminates the backlog of untested and unanalyzed DNA evidence collected in rape kits. DNA identifies the perpetrator and frees those who might be wrongfully accused. Too often, survivors had to wait on the results of their rape kit, leaving them without justice. Not knowing their perpetrator, they lived in fear that their perpetrator would strike again. The Debbie Smith Act changed that by providing much-needed resources to process DNA evidence and add the samples to the national DNA database. The act was named after Debbie Smith, who in 1989 was robbed and raped by a masked stranger at gunpoint at her home in Williamsburg, Virginia. She reported the crime and consented to a sexual assault forensic exam. DNA was collected, but it took more than six years for the perpetrator to be identified. This was because at the time, so many offenders were already in prison. It took time to collect and match the DNA samples to samples from other crime scenes already recorded in the national DNA database. In July 1995, a forensic science lab determined that her perpetrator's DNA matched that of Norman Jimmerson. It was a cold hit, which means that crime scene DNA is matched to a perpetrator or is matched to DNA from another crime scene. At the time, Jimmerson was behind bars for previously abducting two other females. He was convicted and received two life terms and 186 years. Smith went on to create H-E-A-R-T (Hope Exists After Rape Trauma). The organization strives to enact state and federal legislation to help reduce DNA testing backlogs in state labs. Its efforts led to the Debbie Smith Act of 2004.

The Importance of Self-Care

Supporting survivors takes effort and can be overwhelming at times. If you don't practice self-care regularly, a secondary effect, or vicarious trauma, could occur. This is the transference of trauma from survivors to those who are supporting them. Symptoms can include anxiety, depression, fatigue, and fear. The possibility of experiencing secondary trauma doesn't mean you should stop being an ally or advocate. It just means that you need to take deliberate steps to refresh your body, mind, and spirit. This could mean going for a run, planting succulents, laughing it up with a buddy, or settling in with popcorn and a favorite book. However you practice self-care, keep it up so you can be rejuvenated and ready to continue your important efforts of support and creating a society free from sexual violence.

Glossary

Alzheimer's disease A disease that changes brain tissue, thus affecting the memory and mental capabilities of older people.

assault The physical attack on someone by another person.

battery The unlawful act of beating or using force on someone.

call-and-response The method of asking a question or making a statement, with a group of people offering an immediate response.

catcalling The act of calling out to a person with harassing threats or sexually explicit suggestions.

clinical social worker A trained professional who diagnoses and treats one's mental health.

covert Secret and concealed behavior.

defamation The act of publicly sharing false statements about someone that could harm the person's reputation.

dementia A condition in which the brain has a deteriorating ability to reason, remember, or think.

dialect The use of regional grammar, pronunciation, and vocabulary varieties in one language.

flashback A memory of past traumas that seems as if it's taking place in the present.

gender inequity The unequal treatment between women and men.

lethargy A state of feeling sluggish and unenergetic.

misogyny A general hatred of women.

monogamous The state of either being married to one person or having only one sexual partner at a time.

polyamorous The state of having multiple, open romantic and/or sexual relationships at one time.

pregenual anterior cingulate cortex (pgACC) A part of the brain that plays a central role in cognition, including decision making, empathy, emotion, and impulse control.

psychiatrist A trained medical doctor who treats mental, emotional, or behavioral disorders and can prescribe medication.

psychologist A trained professional who uses behavioral interventions to treat patients for emotional and mental suffering.

psychotherapist A trained psychiatrist, psychologist, or social worker who treats individuals, couples, groups, or families for mental or emotional disorders.

self-harm The act of bruising, cutting, or hitting oneself, often in secret.

sodomy The act of anal and/or oral sexual activity.

trafficked The act of selling or trading illegal goods or people.

watershed A ridge that divides one area from another.

Loveisrespect
PO Box 161810
Austin, TX 78716
(866) 331-9474
Text: loveis to 22522
Website: http://www.loveisrespect.org
Facebook: @loveisrespectpage
Instagram: @loveisrespectofficial
Twitter: @loveisrespect
YouTube: loveisrespect
A project of the National Domestic Violence
Hotline, Loveisrespect helps teens and young
adults understand what is and isn't a healthy
relationship and offers one-on-one crisis
support and advocacy for those who are in
abusive relationships.

MaleSurvivor
PO Box 276
Long Valley, NJ 07853
Website: https://www.malesurvivor.org/index.php
Facebook: @MaleSurvivor
Twitter: @MaleSurvivorORG
Email: canderson@malesurvivor.org
Since 1995, MaleSurvivor has worked for the

prevention, healing, and elimination of sexual victimization of men of all ages. It offers support, treatment, research, education, advocacy, and activism.

Native Youth Sexual Health Network (NYSHN)
2345 Yonge Street
PO Box 26069 Broadway
Toronto, ON, Canada M4P 0A8
Website: http://nativeyouthsexualhealth.com
Facebook: The Native Youth Sexual Health Network
Instagram: @nyshn
Twitter: @NYSHN
YouTube: NativeYouthSexualHealthNetwork
The NYSHN is an organization facilitated by and for indigenous youth ages thirty and under. It focuses on sexual and reproductive health, justice, and rights for those living in North America.

NO MORE
45 W. Thirty-Sixth Street
New York, NY 10018
Website: https://nomore.org
Facebook and Twitter: @NOMORE.org
Instagram: @nomoreorg

YouTube: No More

NO MORE is a national public awareness and
engagement movement committed to ending
sexual assault and domestic violence. Its symbol
is available for individuals, corporations, and
organizations to use in their commitment to
the cause.

1in6: Resources for Men Who Experienced
Childhood Sexual Abuse

PO Box 222033

Santa Clarita, CA 91322

(800) 656-HOPE (4673)

Website: https://1in6.org

Facebook, Instagram, and Twitter: @1in6org

YouTube: 1in6

Email: info@1in6.org

This organization helps men who have
experienced childhood abuse and sexual
assault. Its services include a 24/7 online help
line and free and confidential weekly online
support groups for survivors.

Rape, Abuse & Incest National Network (RAINN)
1220 L Street NW, Suite 505

Washington, DC 20005

(800) 656-HOPE (4673)

Website: https://www.rainn.org

Facebook: @rainn01

Instagram and Twitter: @rainn

YouTube: RAINN01

Email: talk@rainn.org

RAINN offers survivors of sexual violence a
    hotline, victim services, public education, and
    consulting services. It works with state and federal
    governments to create public policy changes for
    safer communities and survivor support.

SACHA Sexual Assault Centre

75 MacNab Street S., 3rd Floor

Hamilton, ON, Canada L8P 3C1

(905) 525-4162

Website: http://sacha.ca/home

Facebook: @sacha.hamont

Twitter: @SACHAhamont

Email: crickett@sacha.ca

A feminist, nonprofit, community-based
    organization, SACHA supports survivors of
    sexual assault and works to stop violence and

oppression. Its 24/7 hotline is available in more than three hundred languages.

SafeBAE
(917) 449-8708
Website: http://www.safebae.org
Facebook: @safebae.org
Instagram and Twitter: @safe_bae
Email: shael@safebae.org
As a student-focused, survivor-driven organization, SafeBAE educates students about sexual consent, bystander intervention, dating violence, and more.

Trevor Project
PO Box 69232
West Hollywood, CA 90069
(866) 488-7386
Website: https://www.thetrevorproject.org
Facebook: @TheTrevorProject
Instagram and Twitter: @TrevorProject
The Trevor Project is a crisis intervention nonprofit specifically addressing the needs of LGBTQ young people.

For Further Reading

Byers, Ann. *Sexual Assault and Abuse* (Confronting Violence Against Women). New York, NY: Rosen Publishing, 2016.

Clark, Annie E., and Andrea L. Pino. *We Believe You: Survivors of Campus Sexual Assault Speak Out.* New York, NY: Holt Paperback, 2016.

Henneberg, Susan. *I Have Been Raped. Now What?* (Teen Life 411). New York, NY: Rosen Publishing, 2016.

Hurt, Avery Elizabeth. *Coping with Hate and Intolerance* (Coping). New York, NY: Rosen Publishing, 2018.

Klein, Rebecca. *Rape and Sexual Assault: Healing and Recovery* (Helpline: Teen Issues and Answers). New York, NY: Rosen Publishing, 2014.

La Bella, Laura. *Stalking* (Confronting Violence Against Women). New York, NY: Rosen Publishing, 2016.

Mooney, Carla. *Everything You Need to Know About Sexual Consent* (The Need to Know Library). New York, NY: Rosen Publishing, 2018.

Staley, Erin. *Defeating Stress and Anxiety* (Effective Survival Strategies). New York, NY: Rosen Publishing, 2016.

Bibliography

Canadian Women's Foundation. "Fact Sheet Sexual Assault and Harassment." Retrieved September 2, 2018. https://www.canadianwomen.org /wp-content/uploads/2017/09/Facts-About -Sexual-Assault-and-Harassment.pdf.

Centers for Disease Control and Prevention. "Sexual Violence Prevention." April 5, 2018. https://www.cdc.gov/features/sexualviolence.

Dockterman, Eliana. "'I Was Angry.' Taylor Swift on What Powered Her Sexual Assault Testimony." *Time*, December 6, 2017. http://time.com /5049659/taylor-swift-interview-person-of-the -year-2017.

Drysdale, Jennifer. "Terry Crews Opens Up About His Alleged Sexual Assault While Testifying Before Senate." ETOnline, June 26, 2018. https://www.etonline.com/terry-crews-opens -up-about-his-alleged-sexual-assault-while -testifying-before-senate-105027.

Ellsberg, Michael. "Affirmative Consent and Erotic Tension." January 24, 2015. http://www.ellsberg .com/affirmative-consent-and-erotic-tension.

Government of Canada Department of Justice. "Bill C-46: Records Applications Post-Mills, a Caselaw

Review." Retrieved September 2, 2018. http://
www.justice.gc.ca/eng/rp-pr/csj-sjc/ccs-ajc
/rr06_vic2/p3_4.html#f98.

Indian Law Resource Center. "Ending Violence
Against Native Women." Retrieved September
23, 2108. http://indianlaw.org/issue/ending
-violence-against-native-women.

Judd, Ashley. "How Online Abuse of Women Has
Spiraled out of Control." TEDWomen 2016,
October 2016. https://www.ted.com/talks
/ashley_judd_how_online_abuse_of_women
_has_spiraled_out_of_control?language
=en#t-958844.

National Coalition Against Domestic Violence.
"National Statistics." Retrieved September 19,
2018. https://ncadv.org/statistics#factsheets.

Nebehay, Stephanie. "Rape Used as Wide-Scale
Weapon of War in Syria: UN Report." *Toronto
Globe and Mail*, March 15, 2018. https://
www.theglobeandmail.com/canada/article
-rape-used-as-wide-scale-weapon-of-war-in
-syria-un-report.

NO MORE. "Know the Facts." Retrieved
September 16, 2018. https://nomore.org
/learn/resources.

Nursing Home Abuse Guide. "Elder Sexual Abuse."
Retrieved September 20, 2018. http://www
.nursinghomeabuseguide.org/sexual-abuse.

Parshall, Helen. "Sexual Assault Awareness Month
2018." HRC, April 5, 2018. https://www.hrc.org
/blog/sexual-assault-awareness-month-2018.

Rape, Abuse & Incest National Network. "The
Criminal Justice System: Statistics." Retrieved
September 15, 2018. https://www.rainn.org
/statistics/criminal-justice-system.

Rape, Abuse & Incest National Network. "Scope of
the Problem: Statistics." Retrieved September
23, 2018. https://www.rainn.org/statistics/scope
-problem.

Rape, Abuse & Incest National Network. "What
Is a Rape Kit?" Retrieved September 15, 2018.
https://www.rainn.org/articles/rape-kit.

Rollin, Jennifer. "3 Things Survivors of Sexual
Assault Need to Know." *Psychology Today*, June
7, 2016. https://www.psychologytoday.com
/us/blog/mindful-musings/201606/3-things
-survivors-sexual-assault-need-know.

US Department of Justice. "The Dru Sjodin Story."
NSOPW. Retrieved August 6, 2018. https://
www.nsopw.gov/en/Home/DruSjodin.

Vrangalova, Zhana. "Everything You Need to Know About Consent That You Never Learned in Sex Ed." *Teen Vogue*, April 18, 2016. https://www.teenvogue.com/story/consent-how-to.

World Health Organization. *The Global Status Report on Violence Prevention 2014*. Geneva, Switzerland: World Health Organization, 2014.

Index

About the Author

Erin Staley is a copywriter within the Student Affairs Division of the University of California, Riverside. Her print and online materials share the mission and resources of student support departments, including ethnic and gender programs and CARE (Campus Advocacy, Resources & Education), an intervention and prevention support program committed to ending sexual violence.

Photo Credits

Cover Thanasis Zovoilis/Moment/Getty Images; p. 5 Drew Angerer/Getty Images; p. 6 Ian West/PA Images/Getty Images; p. 7 Bloomberg/Getty Images; p. 10 MinDof/Shutterstock.com; p. 12 LightField Studios/Shutterstock.com; p. 16 © iStockphoto.com /MonicaNinker; p. 19 John Roman Images/Shutterstock.com; p. 23 © iStockphoto.com/ljubaphoto; p. 25 Theo Wargo Getty Images; p. 31 Rick Madonik/Toronto Star/Getty Images; p. 34 © iStockphoto.com/tommaso79; p. 36 Dave Allocco /The LIFE Picture Collection/Getty Images; p. 39 EvGavrilov /Shutterstock.com; pp. 41, 56 © AP Images; p. 45 cunaplus /Shutterstock.com; p. 49 Christian Science Monitor/Getty Images; p. 54 Mark Burnett/Alamy Stock Photo; p. 61 Jeff Kowalsky/AFP /Getty Images; p. 67 © iStockphoto.com/monkeybusinessimages; pp. 71, 77 Dean Drobot/Shutterstock.com; p. 73 Piotr Swat /Shutterstock.com; p. 83 Avivi Aharon/Shutterstock.com; p. 87 Sundry Photography/Shutterstock.com; p. 89 Frazer Harrison /Getty Images.

Design and Layout: Nicole Russo-Duca; Editor: Elissa Petruzzi; Photo Researcher: Nicole DiMella